Valentines Day Activity Book for Kids

My Day Books

Copyright 2014

First Printed January 9, 2015

Solve the puzzles

Spot 9 Differences

Spot 7 differences

Spot 10 differences

Spot 10 differences

Spot 10 differences

Spot 10 differences

Spot 10 differences

Spot 10 differences

All the pictures are the same except for one. Find it.

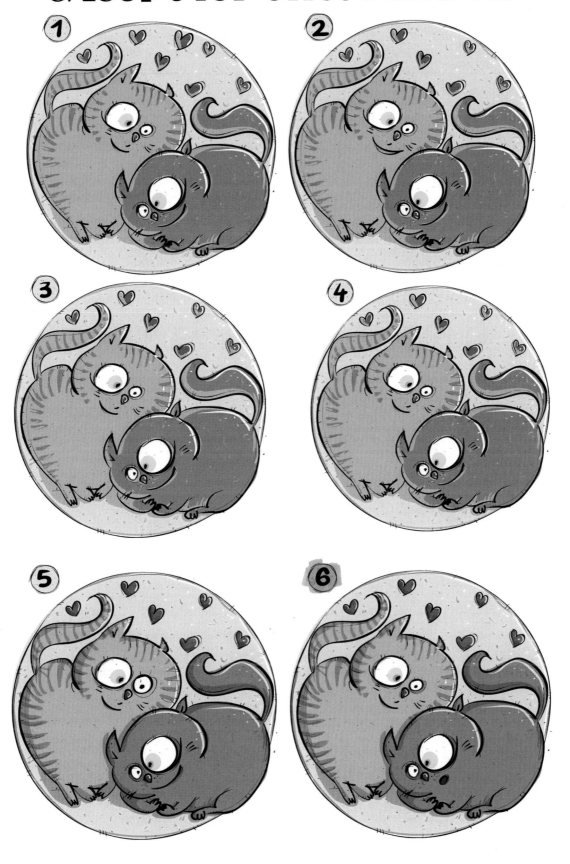

All the pictures are the same except for one. Find it.

Find the two wrong pictures in the list.

Find the two wrong pictures in the list.

Solve the maze.

Solve the maze.

Solve the maze.

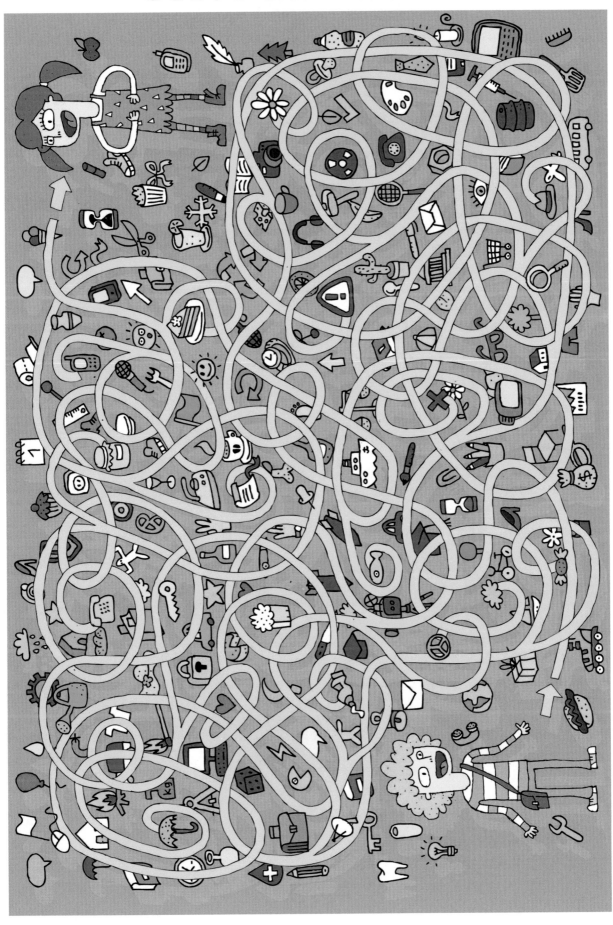

Solve the maze.

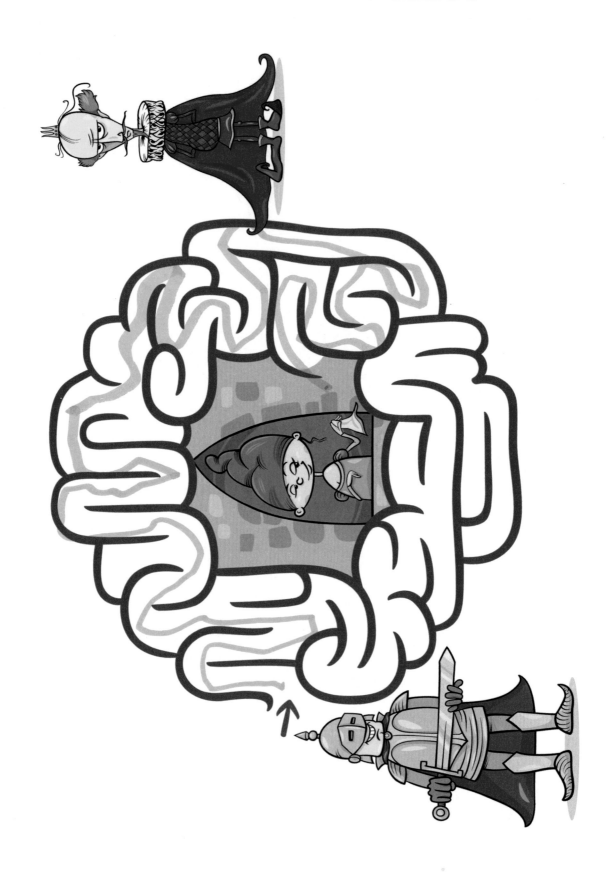

Solve the maze

Solve the Puzzle

Solve the maze

Solve the maze

Match the pictures to their shadows

Match the pictures to their shadows

FILL-IN (or CRISS-CROSS) CROSSWORD PUZZLE

Fill in the blanks with the words: ADMIRATION, ADORER, AMORETTO, BESTMAN, BRIDE, CARESS, CONSTANCY, COUPLE, CUPID, DATING, ENGAGEMENT, EYRE, GIMP, GLAD, GROOM, HEARTEN, HEDGES, HUGS, ISEULT, JULIET, KISS, LYRE, MEALS, ODE, PASSIONS, PENELOPE, PRESENTS, QUEEN, RENDEZVOUS, RING, ROMANCE, ROMEO, ROSE, RYE, SCENTS, SHY, SYMPATHY, TENDER, TIER, TRISTAN, TULLE, ULYSSES, UNISON, WEDDING.

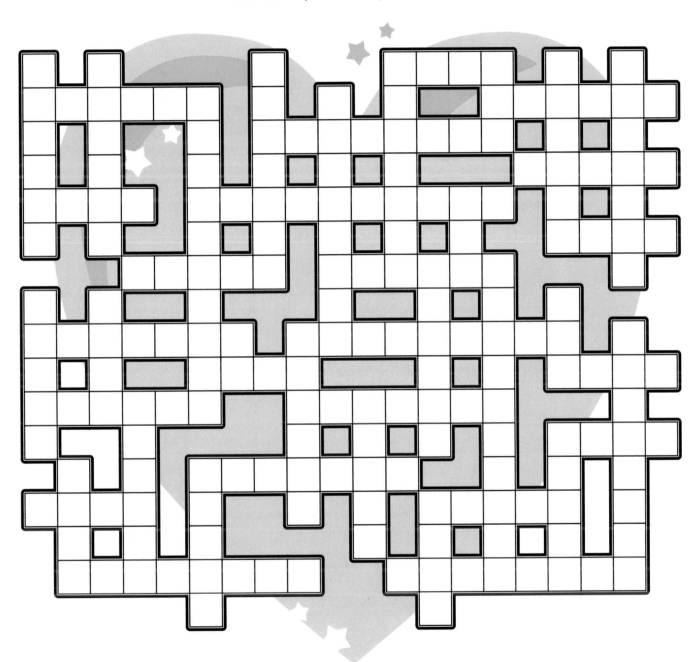

Solutions

Spot 9 Differences

Spot 7 differences

Spot 10 differences

Spot 10 differences

Spot 10 differences

Spot 10 differences

Spot 10 differences

Spot 10 differences

All the pictures are the same except for one. Find it.

All the pictures are the same except for one. Find it.

Find the two wrong pictures in the list.

Find the two wrong pictures in the list.

Solve the maze.

Solve the maze.

Solve the maze.

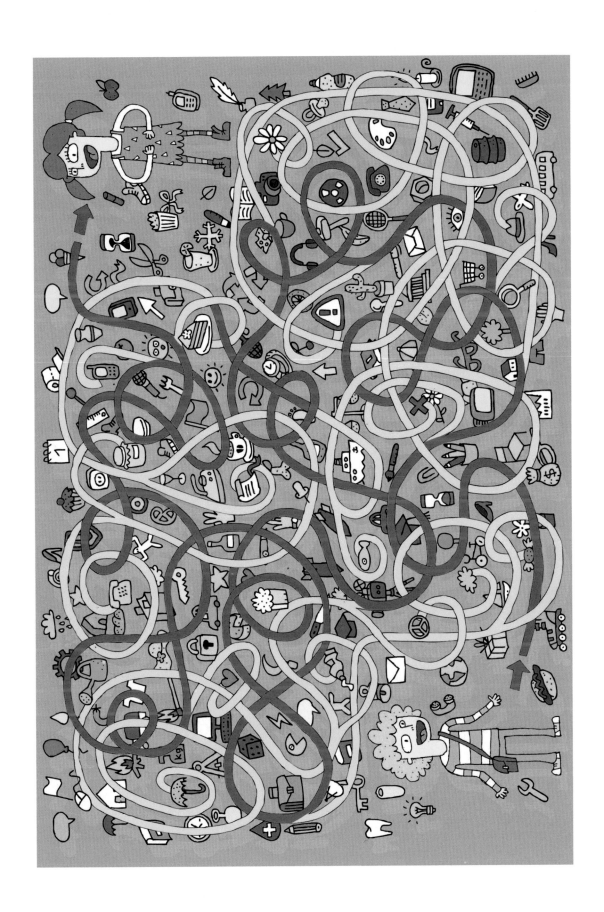

Solve the maze.

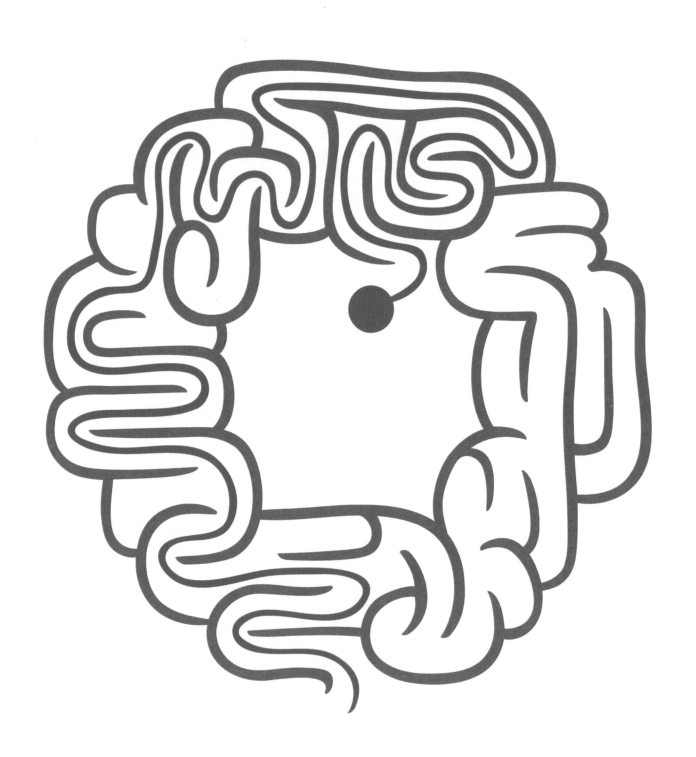

Solve the maze

Solve the Puzzle

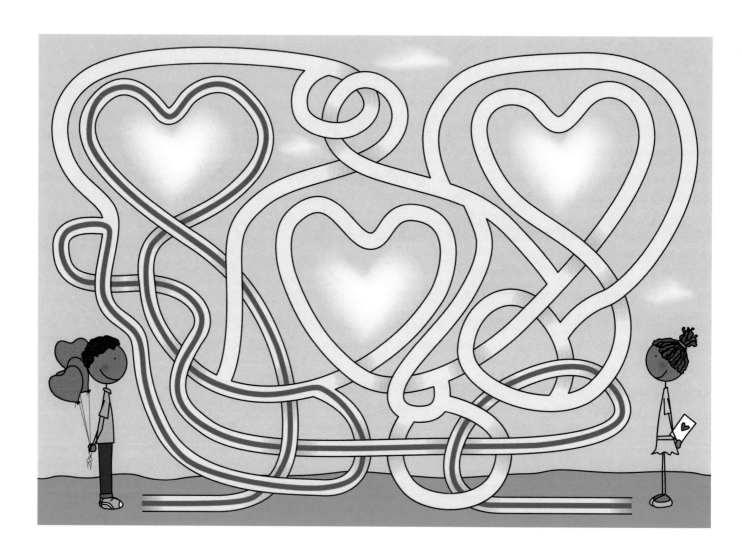

Solve the maze

Solve the maze

Match the pictures to their shadows

ANSWER: _____ 1 - 7, 3 - 4, 6 - 5, 8 - 2

Match the pictures to their shadows

ANSWER:

1 - 2, 4 - 7, 5 - 10, 8 - 3, 9 - 6.

FILL-IN (or CRISS-CROSS) CROSSWORD PUZZLE

Fill in the blanks with the words: ADMIRATION, ADORER, AMORETTO, BESTMAN, BRIDE, CARESS, CONSTANCY, COUPLE, CUPID, DATING, ENGAGEMENT, EYRE, GIMP, GLAD, GROOM, HEARTEN, HEDGES, HUGS, ISEULT, JULIET, KISS, LYRE, MEALS, ODE, PASSIONS, PENELOPE, PRESENTS, QUEEN, RENDEZVOUS, RING, ROMANCE, ROMEO, ROSE, RYE, SCENTS, SHY, SYMPATHY, TENDER, TIER, TRISTAN, TULLE, ULYSSES, UNISON, WEDDING.

S	J					B			H	U	G	S		A		W	
C	O	U	P	L	E		B		A		E		H	E	D	G	E	S
E	L			N		S	Y	M	P	A	T	H	Y		O		D	
N	I			G		T		O		R			B	R	I	D	E	
T	I	E	R		A	D	M	I	R	A	T	I	O	N		E		I
S	T			A		G	A		E		E	D			R	I	N	G
		Q	U	E	E	N		T	E	N	D	E	R			G	
C		L		M			T		A		E		R			
U	L	Y	S	S	E	S	C	O	N	S	T	A	N	C	Y	P
P	R		N	O	R	A		I		D		E	Y	R	E
I	S	E	U	L	T	R	O	M	A	N	C	E		E
D		N			R	E	E	G	Z	R	O	S	E
G	I		T	R	I	S	T	A	N	V	O	E
K	I	S	S	U		S	L	G	R	O	O	M	N
M	O		L			S	L	U	E	T
P	E	N	E	L	O	P	E	P	A	S	S	I	O	N	S
		L				A	D

Made in the USA
Middletown, DE
12 February 2017